CHRISTMAS
Program Builder
No. 46

A Collection of Graded Resources for the
Creative Program Planner

Compiled by Paul M. Miller

For the most practical use of this material, it is
suggested that at least three copies of this book
be purchased. Because it is copyrighted material,
no part can be copied in any way.

LILLENAS PUBLISHING COMPANY
Kansas City, MO 64141

God's Gift

Good news! Good news!
Christ is born,
God's gift to us
This Christmas morn.

—Robert Colbert

The Christmas Star

I am the Christmas Star,
Shining, shining down.
I tell of Jesus' birth,
And shine His love around.

—Janet S. Teitsort

Christmas Blessings

May you have much happiness
On this Christmas Day.
And may God keep you
And bless you in every way!

—Evangeline Carey

Not Sure

I was not sure that I
Could come up here today,
But Dad said, "TRY,"
So (pause), here I am to say,
"HAVE A HAPPY CHRISTMAS DAY!"

—Helen Kitchell Evans

Joyful Christmas

I like big presents *(show size)*,
I like little presents too *(show size)*,
But the best present of all
God gave to me *(point to self)*,
God gave to you *(point to
congregation)*.

—Helen Kitchell Evans

A Little Kid

I'm just a little kid,
But guess what I can do,
Wish Merry Christmas *(Child points
finger, moving it in clockwise
manner)*
To you, and you, and you!

—Robert Colbert

The Christmas Key

*(Child carries a large key made from
cardboard.)*

I have the key for Christmas *(holds
up key)*.
It opens KINDNESS, PEACE,
and LOVE;
It opens the door where Jesus lives
In heaven up above.

—Helen Kitchell Evans

2

Security Blanket

Baby Jesus cold
  As He can be.
He needs the blanket
  I take with me.
    —Margaret Primrose

Don't Crowd Him Out

With all the hurry and the haste,
  The pleasure and the joys,
Excitement found in every place,
  The things we all enjoy.
Take time to honor Christ, the Lord.
  Don't crowd Him from His day.
Make room for Him within your life,
  Invite Him in to stay.
    —Cora Owen

Such a Thrill

It's such a thrill
  On Christmas morn,
To know that Christ
  Was truly born.
    —Robert Colbert

Christmas Is Special

May the specialness of Christmas
  Be real to you this year
As you see how much God loved us
When He sent His Son so dear.
    —Brenda Wood

Christmas Is

Christmas is:
  Peace, love, and glory incline.
Christmas is:
  Joy, laughter, and mercy divine.
Christmas is:
  Gifts, giving, and celebration.
Christmas is:
  God, man, and jubilation.
    —Terisha Younger

May God Bless You at Christmastime!

Jesus brings that special peace to
  earth,
  The Christmas season through,
May He bring His special peace
  Especially to you!
    —Evangeline Carey

The Baby We Love

Sleep, little Baby Jesus,
  Sleep on Your bed of hay;
At Christmas we always see You
  As the Baby we love today.
    —Helen Kitchell Evans

Big Wishes

Big people have big wishes
  But even though I am small
I have a wish that is the biggest
(Open arms to congregation)—
  The biggest wish of all!
HAVE A MERRY CHRISTMAS!
    —Helen Kitchell Evans

A Treasure

It's fun to save something you like.
  It becomes a treasure.
But there is one thing I know
  We can never measure.
That is the love of Jesus,
  His love for you and for me,
Today, tomorrow, forever—
  Throughout eternity.
    —Helen Kitchell Evans

Behold the Manger

May our eyes behold the manger,
  Where our Lord and Savior lay;
As we kneel to worship Him,
  On this blessed Christmas Day.
    —Robert Colbert

Surprises

(CHILD 1 *enters on tiptoe with large wrapped gift.*)

CHILD 1:
Shhhh. I have this gift for Daddy.
    It's been hidden on a shelf.
I hope he likes it very much,
    'Cuz I wrapped it up myself.

(Exits)

(CHILD 2 *enters on tiptoe with present.*)

CHILD 2:
Shhhh. I have a Christmas secret.
    It's for my sister Janey Sue.
I cannot tell you what it is,
    But I'll give you just one clue.

(CHILD 2 *rocks arms as if holding a baby doll, then exits.*)

(CHILD 3 *enters on tiptoe with wrapped gift.*)

CHILD 3:
Shhhh. I want to tell mama "thank you,"
    For all the things she is.
Our family is the best in town,
    'Cuz Mom is such a whiz.

—*Paul Medford*

Good News

Glad tidings of great joy,
    Are what the angels brought.
The best news ever heard—
    See what our God has wrought.
The GREAT event of time,
    It has no parallel.
For God became a man,
    And came to earth to dwell.

—*Cora Owen*

Give Him Praise

In Bethlehem
A King is born
Let's give Him
Praise today,
And bid His peace
Our heart to enter
Forevermore to stay.

—*Robert Colbert*

May God Bless Your Christmas!

May this holy season
    Bring a special joy just for YOU,
Not only at Christmas,
    But all the New Year through!

—*Evangeline Carey*

Ages 6-8

The Best Gift

My name is on this package.
I wonder what is in it—
A game, a toy, or clothing?
I'll know in just a minute.

It will not be the best gift
Of all that I've received,
For Jesus gave eternal life
The moment I believed.

—*Margaret Primrose*

Getting Ready for Christmas

Mommy's baking cookies
And Daddy's building toys.
Grandma's knitting mittens
For homeless girls and boys.

I'd really like to help
And not get in the way;
But even if I can't,
There's something I can say:
"MERRY CHRISTMAS."

—*Margaret Primrose*

We All Do Our Part

Mommy makes a lot of goodies
And wraps the presents up.
Daddy buys the Christmas tree
And puts the star on top.

Brother helps him string the lights,
And hand the sparkly bulbs
I put the little angels on
And our puppy wrecks them all!

—*Marita Root*

An Angel Proclaimed

Good news from heaven
Came down to earth,
At the Savior's
Holy birth.
An angel proclaimed
That Christ was born,
Upon this blessed
Christmas morn.

—*Robert Colbert*

Go Safely Home

We loved having you here today *(or tonight)*
You were so nice to listen.
We hope you had a lot of fun.
Perhaps a tear did glisten.
Depart with blessings from our God,
Go safely on your way.
And if you meet someone alone,
Remember Christmas Day.

—*Judith McFerren*

Take a Stand

At this blessed Christmastime
Let Jesus be our Guide;
Let's face the world and say,
"I'm on Jesus' side!"

Let's be truly ready
To spread the gospel far;
Be ready when our Savior calls,
Be ready where we are.

—*Helen Kitchell Evans*

Celebrate

We came here to celebrate.
  The reason, I am told,
Is a blessed event that happened
  Far away, a long time ago.

"Jesus was born in Bethlehem,"
  In a manger, the Bible does say.
"Jesus was born in Bethlehem,"
  We celebrate today.

Celebrate the name of Jesus,
  Celebrate His birth.
Hallelujah, Wonderful Savior,
  Bringing peace on earth.
            —*Theodoris G. Smith*

Sit Back and Relax

We have planned a real nice program.
  We hope you will agree
After you have seen
  All that you will see.

So sit back and relax,
  Parents, don't you fret!
We've worked very hard *(pause)*
  And we think we won't forget!
            —*Helen Kitchell Evans*

What Christmas Is

Candles and tinsel,
  Ribbon and holly,
Games, books, and cards,
  Maybe a dolly.

These don't make Christmas.
  It came from above
When God sent a Baby
  To show us His love.
            —*Margaret Primrose*

A Pledge

CHILD 1: When I grow up I want to be
            A Christian,
              strong and true.

CHILD 2: I hope to be like Him
            In everything I do.

BOTH: So on this Christmas Day
            We pledge to each one
              here;
            We will give our lives to
              Jesus
            Each day of every year.
            —*Helen Kitchell Evans*

An Announcement

Ladies and gentlemen;
  Mothers, dads, and brothers.
Christmas greetings to you all,
  As well as to you others.

We are your kids,
You love us all.
And now it's time to say,
"Welcome to our yuletide do,
We're glad you're here today.
            —*Paul Medford*

Happy Birthday

Grandma baked a special cake
 That's pretty as can be.
It's not for Grandpa's birthday,
 And it's not for you and me.

She made the cake to honor
 The birthday of a King,
And though you do not see Him,
 Join hands with me and sing.

Happy birthday to You;
 Happy birthday to You;
Happy birthday, King Jesus,
 We'll love and serve You.

—Margaret Primrose

He's Here

I'd like to be a shepherd boy,
 And hear the angels sing;
Then hurry off to Bethlehem
 To see the newborn King.

But maybe I would fall asleep
 Before the sky turns bright,
Or maybe I would have to stay,
 And watch the sheep all night.

But why spend time imagining?
 He's here with me today,
And I can always talk to Him
 At home, at school, at play.

—Margaret Primrose

A Bed of Hay

Grandpa's barn is smelly.
 It has some spiders too.
The hay is full of dust
 That makes me go "Kerchoo!"

The pony snorts at me
 If I'm nearby at play.
I wonder how he'd like
 A baby in his hay.

But Baby Jesus slept
 Where sheep and cattle fed.
I think of that at night
 When I am snug in bed.

—Margaret Primrose

One Small Birthday

One small birthday
 Caused joy to abound;
One small birthday
 Shed light all around.

One small baby
 Brought wise men to the King;
One small baby
 Caused the angels to sing.

The Christ child was that baby
 That changed all the earth;
And gave hope for salvation
 By His humble birth.

—Helen Kitchell Evans

Welcome

Welcome every sir and madam
  Welcome every girl and boy
Welcome to our merry program
  We wish you Christmas joy.

We welcome each of you the same,
  Those from near and those from
  far.
We welcome all of you who came,
  Those by foot and those by car.

We're happy to see you this
  Christmas Day
You're welcome, we proclaim!
To each and every friend we say
  You're welcome in Jesus' name.

—Theodoris G. Smith

O Holy Night in Bethlehem

CHILD 1:
  The heavenly angels sang for joy,

CHILD 2:
  They were happy on that night,

CHILD 3:
  The night when all the stars shone,

CHILD 4:
  So clear, so large, so bright!

CHILD 5:
  The night when God sent to us
    His precious gift of love;

CHILD 6:
  His only Son, our Savior,
    Came from heaven above.

ALL:
  O holy night in Bethlehem,
    How wonderful to know
  A Savior born to show us
    How to live and grow.

—Helen Kitchell Evans

The Shepherd

CHILD 1:
  Long ago the shepherds
    Watched their flocks by night;
  Shepherds care for each lamb
    So if one gets out of sight
  They go with their shepherd's
    crook
  And save them from a fall.
  Yes, shepherds care for all.

CHILD 2:
  Jesus is like a shepherd,
    For He watches each one here;
  Each person in the world
    Jesus holds very dear.
  Let's remember Jesus does care
  And that we can speak to Him in
    prayer.

BOTH:
  Shepherd Jesus, now we pray
    Be with each one this Christmas
    Day.

—Helen Kitchell Evans

May God Light Your Christmas!

CHILD 1:
  May God light your Christmas
    With peace and joy too,
  So that you're blessed each day
    In all that you do!

CHILD 2:
  May God light your Christmas,
    All season long,
  So that you praise Him
    With a merry song!

CHILD 3:
  May God light your Christmas
    And send happiness your way,
  May you think on Jesus
    Each and every day!

—Evangeline Carey

God's Greatest Gift

The stable had no carpet,
　No holly on the door,
No strings of glowing lights,
　No games and toys galore.

There were no ribboned gifts
　Beneath a Christmas tree,
No stacks of greeting cards
　Addressed to you and me.

But this is where God gave
　The greatest gift of all,
Because the gift was Jesus,
　The Baby in the stall.

—Margaret Primrose

Little Lambs

CHILD 1:
　This night is strange, so quiet
　　and so cold.
　And here we huddle within our
　　fold.

CHILD 2:
　The shepherds kept us safe from
　　harm,
　But when they left we were so
　　alarmed!

CHILD 3:
　The sky grew suddenly, strangely
　　bright,
　And angel voices filled the night.

CHILD 4:
　Glory to God, those angels sang,
　Peace on earth, their voices rang.

CHILD 5:
　"The Savior is born," that's what
　　they said,
　He's lying in a straw-filled
　　manger bed.

CHILD 6:
　The shepherds went to see this
　　wonderful sight,
　We're alone but not afraid on
　　this special night.

ALL:
　Jesus is born and brings hope and
　　light,
　Celebrate God's love, the first
　　Christmas night.
　Happy birthday, Baby Jesus!

—Sharon Kaye Kiesel

Little Lambs of Jesus

CHILD 1: Shepherds care for their
　　lambs night and day.

CHILD 2: Jesus Christ cares for us
　　the same way.

CHILD 1: If we should wander,

CHILD 2: If we should stray,

CHILD 4: Then our Savior will say:

CHILD 3: One of My lambs is lost,
　　I fear.

CHILD 4: Every child in the world
　　brings God cheer.

CHILD 1: Jesus loves every one.

CHILD 2: Each child is very dear.

CHILD 3: Jesus wants all of us near.

—Helen Kitchell Evans

The Angels Are Here

The angels are in town tonight
   Their carols fill the air;
Lovely voices, tiny voices
   Spreading joy everywhere.

Yes, I know these angels,
   They are friends and family
Who come upon my porch
   And each year sing for me.

They haven't come from heaven,
   But God sends them just the same.
And although they are family and
   friends
   They come in His holy name.

          —Helen Kitchell Evans

A Special Gift

I heard about a special gift
   That someone sent our way.
It came to earth from heav'n above
   On that first Christmas Day.

A gift not wrapped in paper
   Or tied up in a bow;
But a gift wrapped up in flesh and
   blood
   Sent many years ago.

Sent not to just one person
   But to all who would receive
A gift whose presence is in one's
   heart
   Not underneath a tree.

A gift to last a lifetime,
   A gift that has no end.
A gift to live within the heart
   And take away our sin.

And all who will receive this gift
   Become the sons of God.
This very special Christmas gift
   Is Jesus Christ the Lord.

          —Brenda Wood

Snowflakes

(Snowflakes enter, slowly twirling about.)

CHILD 1:
   It's Christmastime, see it snow.
   And we snowflakes are on the go.
   We are scattered all over the earth,
   To remind one and all of Jesus'
     birth.

CHILD 2:
   God made us special, don't you see?
   No one looks exactly like you or me,
   He loves us all, every one,
   That's why He sent us His only
     Son.

CHILD 3:
   Do we remind you of the
     Christmas star?
   It led the wise men from afar.
   Each of us twinkles and sparkles
     bright,
   To give the world hope through
     the long winter night.

CHILD 4:
   We sparkle and glitter with light
     from above,
   To remind us all of God's
     special love.
   We shine with the light of Jesus
     the King,
   We give praise to Him who
     created all things.

CHILD 5:
   Shine like us, but in God's holy
     light,
   Be so pretty, clean, and bright.
   Believe on Jesus—He forgives all
     sin,
   Open your heart, and let Jesus in.
(Snowflakes twirl off stage.)

          —Sharon Kaye Kiesel

I'd Like . . .

CHILD 1:

I'd like to ride a camel
  That travels near and far.
Then I'd be like the wise men
  Who saw the big bright star.

CHILD 2:

I'd rather be a shepherd
  And camp beside a spring.
Perhaps I'd see the angels
  And even hear them sing.

CHILD 3:

I'm glad it's Jesus' birthday,
  And I'm a child today.
I'd like to share His story
  With people far away.

CHILD 4:

Let's not waste time just dreaming
  Of what we'd like to do.
We each can tell Him thank You,
  And that's important too.

—Margaret Primrose

The Search for Meaning

CHILD 1:

I asked the clerk,
Who worked in the store,
"What is Christmas about?"
And he replied,
"It's about making money,
And a whole lot more.
It's sales and promotion,
And decorating the floor!"

CHILD 2:

I asked my teacher,
"What is Christmas about?"
She paused and she thought,
"It's about Santa Claus and elves,
Making surprises and doing plays.
You see, it's cut and paste,
That fills all our days."

CHILD 3:

I asked my baby-sitter,
"What is Christmas about?"
She said, "It's baking cookies
And shopping for gifts.
You must be sure
That everything fits!"

CHILD 4:

I asked my folks,
"What is Christmas about?"
But they replied,
"Don't bother us now,
There's parties galore,
And much to do,
And don't forget your chores!"

CHILD 5:

I asked my Sunday School
    teacher,
"What is Christmas about?"
And she told me,
"Love was born
Upon that night.
Angels sang,
It was a heavenly sight!

"A babe in a manger,
Our Savior was He.
He came to earth,
To set us free."

—Janet Teitsort

My Gift for Jesus

I bought a book for Grandma
 And a ball for little Ben;
A bright red tie for Grandpa,
 And Daddy will get a pen.

I got a box of candy
 That I know my mom will like.
Then next I thought of Andy
 And a basket for his bike.

So now I'm out of money
 And there's nothing left for Kim
Except this dirty bunny
 And I know she won't like him.

Well, no; Kim likes the sweater
 I purchased just for me.
I'm sure I'll feel much better
 If I put it 'neath her tree.

I want my friends and brothers
 To like the things I do.
For what we do for others,
 Are gifts to Jesus too.

—Margaret Primrose

The Best Gift

(Four children carry large sheets of poster board decorated according to their verse. The last poster should reverse to a replica of the Bible. An easy way to accomplish this is to staple one large sheet of black poster board to the piece used for the package. Then all you have to do is add the lettering.)

CHILD 1:
 I am the best gift,
  That one can receive
 I cost so much,
  It's hard to believe!

CHILD 2:
 I am the best gift,
  That you'll find under the tree.
 I'm the latest craze on the market,
  Everyone wants one of me!

CHILD 3:
 I am the best gift,
  Get a load of my bow!
 The wrapping's important,
  Everyone should know!

CHILD 4:
 My wrappings are not fancy,
  And I'm free to those who
  believe.
 My cost is not of money,
  But I'm the best gift you'll
  receive,
(Flips over poster to Bible, and says),
 THE SAVIOR,
 MERRY CHRISTMAS!

—Janet Teitsort

What Christmas Means

CHILD 1:
 What does Christmas mean to me?
 Love around our Christmas tree.

CHILD 2:
 What does Christmas mean to me?
 A country that is truly free!

CHILD 3:
 What does Christmas mean to me?
 A time of family loyalty.

CHILD 4:
 What does Christmas mean to me?
 Churches filled with pageantry.

CHILD 5:
 What does Christmas mean to me?
 Food baskets ready for delivery.

CHILD 6:
 What does Christmas mean to me?
 A feeling of great unity.

CHILD 7:
 What does Christmas mean to me?
 A famous day in history.

CHILD 8:

What does Christmas mean to me?
God's Son come to earth in
humility.

ALL:

What does Christmas mean to me?
Jesus died on Calvary!
Salvation there for you and me!
That's what Christmas means
to me!

—*Helen Kitchell Evans*

Christmas Star

CHILD 1:

Star so big, star so bright,
The Christmas star shines tonight.
See it point over hills so far,
Guiding wise men who follow
God's star.

CHILD 2:

The starshine glows from east to
west,
Leading man to the stable blessed.
And to the Baby in the manger
there,
Who is snug and warm, without a
care.

CHILD 3:

The star rests high above
Bethlehem town,
Where the wise men came with
golden crown,
To honor Baby Jesus so gentle
and small,
Who lies there sleeping in a
donkey's stall.

CHILD 4:

Star so big, star so bright,
Remind those of us who are here
tonight,
Christmas is the birthday of
Jesus, our King,
So let us rejoice and let our
praises ring!

—*Sharon Kaye Kiesel*

A Place for Jesus

I counted all the people
That Mother said there'd be
To share our Christmas dinner
And gifts around the tree.

"We still have room," I told her.
"There's something we should do.
Let's set a place for Jesus
For He's invited too."

When Grandma came that morning,
She brought along a boy.
He shared our Christmas dinner
And also got a toy.

"I had a lot of fun today,"
I told my mom that night.
"But Billy sat in Jesus' place.
Would God think that's all right?"

"Oh, yes," said Mother quickly.
"He wouldn't think it's odd.
The things we do for others
Are what we do for God."

—*Margaret Primrose*

Discovery

Camels! You saw camels
Swaying as they lumbered
While the whole town slumbered?
What's so strange in that?

Wise men! Wise men, did you say?
Men of noble graces,
Men from far-off places?
Why would they come here?

Treasures! They brought treasures?
Gold and spice, maybe gem.
Brought them here to Bethlehem?
Why would they do that?

The King? They saw the King?
There's no king in our town,
No one here in royal gown.
Surely you are wrong.

That star! That star led them!
Following it they found Him
With its rays around Him.
I will worship too.

—*Margaret Primrose*

Thanks, God

Thanks for the baby
  Who needed a bed
But slept on the hay
  Where the cattle fed.

Thanks for the angels
  Who came down to earth
To tell the shepherds
  Of Jesus' birth.

Lord, thanks for the star,
  So big and so bright.
The wise men saw it
  And followed its light.

Thanks, God, that Your love
  Is for everyone,
And that's the reason
  You sent us Your Son.

—*Margaret Primrose*

A Christmas Stocking

*(The child carries a large stocking
with "Jesus" written on it in large
stick-on letters. The stocking is car-
ried with the plain side facing the au-
dience. Inside the stocking is a large
construction paper heart.)*

I have a Christmas stocking
  That hangs at home for me;
And every year that stocking
  Is filled with gifts for me.

The stocking in my hand now
  Is meant for someone else.
*(Turns stocking around to show
Jesus' name.)*
I'm the one who's giving now;
  I'm giving Him myself.
(Pulls heart out of stocking.)

—*Judith McFerren*

That Special Day

When days grow short
  And leaves turn brown,
When snow is lying
  On the ground,
A special birthday
  Comes around.
We call it Christmas—
  That's the name
Of the special day
  When Jesus came.
When winter comes,
  And the year is old,
When the birds fly south
  And nights grow cold,
A special story
  Then is told.
We call it Christmas—
  That's the name
Of the special day
  When Jesus came.

—*Wanda M. Trawick*

A Special Guest

I could wish you Merry Christmas
  And a Happy New Year too.
But there is something else tonight
  That I would rather do.

I'd like to give you each a chance
  To meet a special guest.
Someone who says, "Come unto me,
  And I will give you rest."

He lived 2,000 years ago
  And still He lives today.
And to all those who are seeking,
  He says, "I am the way."

Gently knocking on our heart's door
  Jesus seeks to enter in.
If we open the door
  He will take away our sin.

What makes this guest so special
  One cannot help but see—
He loved us all so very much
  He died upon a tree.

He sent us each a letter *(hold up
    Bible),*
  Which tells us of His love.
And He offers us eternal life
  With Him in heaven above.

Tonight as we are gathered here
  We honor this special one.
"For God so loved the world He gave
  His only begotten Son."

  —Brenda Wood

A Birthday Gift

*(Child enters carrying large wrapped
box and sets it on the floor.)*

It's Your birthday, Baby Jesus, I
    wish I could bring,
A golden gift that's fit for a king.
I wish I could bring a pillow for
    Your head—
Or a nice warm blanket for Your
    manger bed.

But I have no money, no silver or
    gold.
And that's not what You want, so
    I've been told.
Yet I can give a gift for You to
see *(remove box lid),*
I'll give You my all, I'll give You
    (step in box)—ME!

  —Sharon Kaye Kiesel

15

Plays and Programs for All Ages

A Little Lamb's Christmas

by Nancy Buscher

The tree was trimmed with paper fans and balls and little trains, and crystal birds and white snowflakes and lots of candy canes. Thin brass designs and golden rope and lights strung carefully and lambs of white and bows of red adorned this cheery tree. Poinsettias sat about the room. The mistletoe was hung, and all was prepared with loving care for Christmas Day to come.

The children yawned and made their way upstairs and into bed. Their parents followed close behind, once their good-nights were said.

The clock struck 10 on Christmas Eve, the clock out in the hall. All were asleep, so no one knew what made the white lamb fall. He bounced past all the strings of lights. He bumped both to and fro, fell past the rope, and balls and birds, and to the floor below.

He sprawled there for a moment, and he shook his head to clear, then paused, and made it to his feet, and looked . . . way . . . back . . . up . . . there.

He'd fallen down through that tall tree. That surely was a fact. But even more importantly, he knew he must get back! He tried to reach the lowest branch, but it was still too high. He tried to climb upon the gifts, but fell with every try.

The ticking of the clock was like the beating of his heart. A growing fear crept into him, into the deepest part.

He first went this way, then went that, but couldn't find a way. The time was short, and drawing nearer, and almost Christmas Day!

He tried to stand on his back hooves. And then he tried to jump. And several times he slipped and fell into a woolen lump. His eyes filled up with hot, wet tears. He brushed them all away. He sat down on the floor distraught, and cried his sheeply way.

The lamb looked past the presents where he saw some piled books. Beside them stood an old white couch, and on and on he looked. The couch sat by a windowsill, which was beside a chair, a table stood just to its right, all laid with Christmas ware. Just then a thought occurred to him! He got right to his feet. He looked again, and then let out a most triumphant bleat. The table stretched for quite a way, ending at the knee of the old desk beside his precious Christmas tree.

His heart now filled with joy and hope. He ran across the floor. He climbed the books, jumped on the couch, and ran on, even more. He reached the window very soon. Onto the sill he hopped. Then dashed away, right to the chair—where suddenly, he stopped. The chair was made of wood, he saw, all waxed and slippery. He must not fall. He knew he must proceed most cautiously. So, step by step he made his way across the chair's curved arm and safely reached the table's top, avoiding, any harm. The table, too, was wooden, but it had a colored mat that ran full length along the top, on which the manger sat.

The lamb drew back. What was this thing? His eyes were opened wide. He peeked around the corner and saw them all inside. The shepherds kneeling by the door, and wise men, there were three. And Joseph knelt. And Mary knelt. Beyond, he couldn't see.

The clock in the hallway struck. And chimes rang all around. The lamb dropped to his knees, startled by the sound. His eyes were closed. He shook with fear. Then he heard someone say, "Don't be afraid. Come closer, Lamb." He knew he must obey.

He opened each eye slowly, and looked around to see. Who had said that? Then he heard, "Please, won't you come to Me?"

All was still and yet he heard soft music far away. Then from the crib there shone a light that made it bright as day. He rose and went toward the light. He paused, and then peeked in. An infant child lay there inside. The Child looked up and grinned.

"I'm very cold," the Child spoke, "I have no winter clothes." The lamb stepped closer and leaning forward, he touched Him with his nose.

He breathed warm breath upon the Babe. The breath rose in the cold, and met the light, and turned into snowflakes of purest gold. They settled down around the Child and covered Him like cloth. The lamb just smiled and blew the breath that made this golden froth.

The Child reached up, and with His hand, He stroked him tenderly.

"I'll grant you any wish," He said. "You've been so kind to Me."

The Babe's eyes closed. He fell asleep, there in His golden bed. The mother, Mary, touched the lamb and kissed him on his head.

"What will it be, this wish of yours, my Son would grant to thee?"

"Please, Ma'am," the lamb spoke, "if He would . . . put me back in the tree."

She patted him. He closed his eyes and smiled most humbly. And when his eyes opened again, he was back in his tree.

The clock struck 12 on Christmas Day. The chimes rang in with glee. And from his place high on a branch, the lamb watched happily.

It's the Best We Have

by Margaret Primrose

Characters:
RANDY
KATIE
MOTHER

(RANDY *looks in boxes and bags on the table. He holds a sweatshirt in front of him.)*

KATIE: What are you doing? You shouldn't be snooping in Mother's Christmas secrets.

RANDY: She left this stuff on the table where anyone can see it. I'm not snooping, am I?

KATIE: You'd say so if I did it.

RANDY: Well, I'll put the shirt back. It really is a nice one. Can't I just try it on?

KATIE: Not until Christmas Eve. That's only one more day. Where do you suppose Mother is?

RANDY: I don't know. She's usually home from work by this time. She must have been here. Maybe she had to go to the store for something for dinner.

KATIE: Not Mother. You know she only shops once a week. She doesn't leave jobs half-done either. Wherever she went, she must have had to hurry.

RANDY: Maybe she left us a note.

KATIE: No, I looked at the bulletin board.

RANDY: Well, that must mean she didn't plan to be gone long. Do you suppose Gram and Grandpa got an earlier flight than they expected? Mother might have gone to the airport to get them.

KATIE: No, travelers are usually late at Christmas. I can't figure this out.

RANDY: Neither can I.

(KATIE *glances out the window.)*

KATIE: There she is.

MOTHER: Hi, kids. Sorry I had to leave in a hurry. I thought I'd be back before you were home from the party. I hope you didn't look at anything on the table.

KATIE: Randy did.

RANDY: Well, I . . . You wouldn't leave things around in plain sight if they were for Christmas, would you?

MOTHER: Not usually, but this time I did.

KATIE: RANDY saw the sweatshirt, but I caught him before he had time to try it on.

MOTHER: Well, it just won't be a surprise tomorrow night.

RANDY: Oh, well. Gram and Grandpa always bring gifts, and I won't know what's in their packages.

MOTHER: I'm sorry to have to tell you this, but your grandparents won't be here this Christmas. The packages will be late because they were not mailed until today.

RANDY: You don't mean it.

KATIE: I can't believe this. Gram and Grandpa always come for Christmas.

MOTHER: There was an emergency in Grandpa's office. He and Grandma had to put off the trip until spring. I know you're disappointed, but you'll be glad to have them when the weather is warmer.

RANDY: I know that, but what is Christmas going to be like without them? Besides, I did all that cleaning in my room to get it ready for them. I even emptied a drawer for their things.

MOTHER: I know, and I appreciate it that you were willing to sleep on the sofa. *(Sighs)* I hate to tell you this, but there's more bad news.

RANDY: Oh, no!

KATIE: What now?

MOTHER: The Martins' house caught fire this afternoon.

RANDY: The firemen got it out, didn't they?

MOTHER: Yes, but not before almost everything burned.

RANDY: That's awful. Jon won't even have any Christmas presents.

KATIE: Is there something we can do to help?

MOTHER: I'm coming to that. Randy, do you suppose you and Jon could each use one end of the sofa? It won't be very comfortable to sleep that way.

RANDY: Wow! That's a great idea. We'll have company for Christmas after all.

MOTHER: Yes, and our best friends, in fact.

KATIE: We don't have a baby bed anymore. What will you do about Andy?

MOTHER: I have an idea. Randy, bring that clean drawer from your room. Katie, get the extra pillow from your bed. I think the baby may be able to get by with them for a crib.

KATIE: Here, Mother. I brought my big doll, too, just so we can try Andy's bed.

RANDY: Here's the drawer.

(RANDY *and* KATIE *put the pillow and doll in the drawer.*)

KATIE: There. I guess that will be better than a manger.

RANDY: It sure will. We're kind of like the owner of the stable when Jesus was born, aren't we?

MOTHER: I hadn't taken time to think about it, but yes, I guess we are. We're offering what we have even though it's not the best.

RANDY: There won't be any wise men to visit us, though. I wish you would come up with a gift for Jon. When will he and the rest of his family get here?

MOTHER: They're trying to take care of the things they can save right now, and the neighbor next door to them invited them to dinner. That gives us a little time to plan, but there really isn't money left to shop for gifts.

KATIE: I have an idea. I got this box of chocolate-covered cherries at the party. I could give them to Jon's parents.

MOTHER: That's a wonderful idea, Katie. I'm proud of you for thinking of it.

RANDY: Uh . . . Mom. That's a neat sweatshirt, but I really do have plenty of clothes. Could we give it to Jon?

MOTHER: Thank you, Randy. I hated to ask you if it would be all right, but I'm glad my little king offered it. The kings who visited Jesus had more costly presents, but the shirt is your best, and that is what's important.

RANDY: But won't the baby get any gifts?

MOTHER: I'm going to share the clothes you wore. There's a special outfit that was too little for you to wear when you received it. Andy will look nice in it.

RANDY: Hey! We're going to have a super Christmas after all. Come on. Let's get the stuff wrapped.

Don't You See?

by Arlys Cauwels

(A rap song for middle ages. They create their own rhythm and movements.)

If Baby Jesus came to our church,
   And cried all through the sermon,
Would you send Him to the nursery
   For His wigglin' and His squirmin'?

Don't you see
   He's around?
Oh, please,
   Don't turn Him down.

If as a lad He came to spend
   This Sabbath day with us,
Would you listen to His teachings,
   Or turn and say, "Oh, hush!"

Don't you see
   He's around?
Oh, please,
   Don't turn Him down.

If as a teen He sang a song
   With quite a different beat,
Would you listen with delight
   Or think He's not too neat?

Don't you see
   He's around?
Oh, please,
   Don't turn Him down.

If as a young man spending time
   In prayer and meditation,

Would you say He was a bum
   Who had no motivation?

Don't you see
   He's around?
Oh, please,
   Don't turn Him down.

If in the end when bruised and
      beaten
   His stand has never wavered,
Would you label Him a radical
   His death you would have favored?

Don't you see
   He's around?
Oh, please,
   Don't turn Him down.

I think the Babe's among us
   For all of us to see.
Do you recognize His presence
   Within your enemy?

Don't you see
   He's around?
Oh, please,
   Don't turn Him down.
Don't you see?
   Don't you see?
Don't you see?

Joyful, Joyful, We Adore You

LINDA LEE JOHNSON

LUDWIG VAN BEETHOVEN

1. Joy - ful, joy - ful, we a - dore You, God of glo - ry, Lord of light;
2. All Your works de - clare Your glo - ry; All cre - a - tion joins to sing.

An - gels lift - ing praise be - fore You Sing thro' - out this ho - ly night.
Praise re - sounds as earth re - joic - es In the birth of Christ, the King.

In a man - ger lies a Ba - by– Child of Mar - y, Son of God.
Shep - herds kneel be - fore the In - fant. Trum - pets sound and an - thems raise

Voic - es joined in joy - ful cho - rus Praise You for Your gift of love.
As with joy our hearts are lift - ed, Joined in won - der, love, and praise.

Jesus Comes, the Heavens Adoring

Advent Hymn

G. THRING

RICHARD H. NEIDERHISER

1. Je - sus came, the heav'ns a - dor - ing, Came with peace from
2. Je - sus comes a - gain in mer - cy, When our hearts are
3. Je - sus comes in joy and sor - row, Shares a - like our
4. Je - sus comes to hearts re - joic - ing, Bring - ing news of
5. Je - sus comes on clouds tri - um - phant, When the heav'ns shall

realms on high; Je - sus came for man's re - demp - tion,
bowed with care; Je - sus comes a - gain in an - swer
hopes and fears; Je - sus comes, what - e'er be - falls us,
sins for - giv'n; Je - sus comes in sounds of glad - ness,
pass a - way; Je - sus comes a - gain in glo - ry,

Low - ly came on earth to die; Al - le - lu - ia!
To an ear - nest heart - felt prayer; Al - le - lu - ia!
Glads our hearts, and dries our tears; Al - le - lu - ia!
Lead - ing souls re - deemed to heav'n: Al - le - lu - ia!
Let us then our hom - age pay, Al - le - lu - ia!

Al - le - lu - ia! Came in deep hu - mil - i - ty.
Al - le - lu - ia! Comes to save us from de - spair.
Al - le - lu - ia! Cheer - ing e'en our fail - ing years.
Al - le - lu - ia! Now the gate of death is riv'n.
Ev - er sing - ing, Till the dawn of end - less day.

The Promise

S. P.

SHIRLEY PORTER

The prom-ise came_____ from long a-go— of a

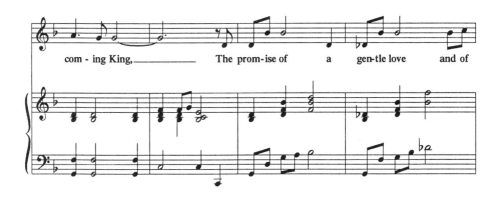

com - ing King,_____ The prom-ise of a gen-tle love and of

peace with-in._____ The prom-ise came____ from heav'n a-bove, and the

world be-held a King. In a sta-ble bare came this gift so rare, and with

joy the an-gels sing: *Group 1* Lit-tle small One, *Group 2* al-le - lu, *Group 1* Ba-by

Group 2 Je-sus, al-le - lu. *All together* Pre-cious Child from God a - bove, do You

know You bring the gift of love,_____ And all heav'n and earth shall praise the

King and the prom-ise You so gent - ly bring?

Group 1

Lit - tle bring? Lit - tle small One, al - le -

lu, Ba - by Je - sus, al - le - lu.

rit.

rit.